ANIMALS
That Make a Difference!

# Prairie Dogs

**Ashley Lee**

Explore other books at:
e WWW.ENGAGEBOOKS.COM

VANCOUVER, B.C.

**e** WWW.ENGAGEBOOKS.COM

*Prairie Dogs: Pre-1*
*Animals That Make a Difference!*
Lee, Ashley, 1995
Text © 2025 Engage Books
Design © 2025 Engage Books

Edited by: A.R. Roumanis, and Ashley Lee
Design by: Mandy Christiansen

Text set in Arial Regular.

FIRST EDITION / FIRST PRINTING

library and archives canada cataloguing in publication

Title: Prairie Dogs / Ashley Lee.
Names: Lee, Ashley, author.
Description: Series statement: Animals that make a difference

Identifiers: Canadiana (print) 20230448542 | Canadiana (ebook) 20230448569
ISBN 978-1-77878-692-1 (hardcover)
ISBN 978-1-77878-701-0 (softcover)

Subjects:
LCSH: Prairie Dogs—Juvenile literature.
LCSH: Human-animal relationships—Juvenile literature.

Classification: LCC QL737.P94 C38 2025 | DDC J599.885—DC23

This project has been made possible in part
by the Government of Canada.

Canada

Prairie dogs are not dogs!

Prairie dogs are
a kind of squirrel.

They do not climb trees like other squirrels.

Prairie dogs are brown or gray.

They have small, round ears.

Prairie dogs eat grass and other plants.

They keep the grass around them short.

Short grass makes it hard for other animals to attack them.

11

Prairie dogs live in North America.

They live in grasslands.

Prairie dogs live in large groups.

These groups are made up of families.

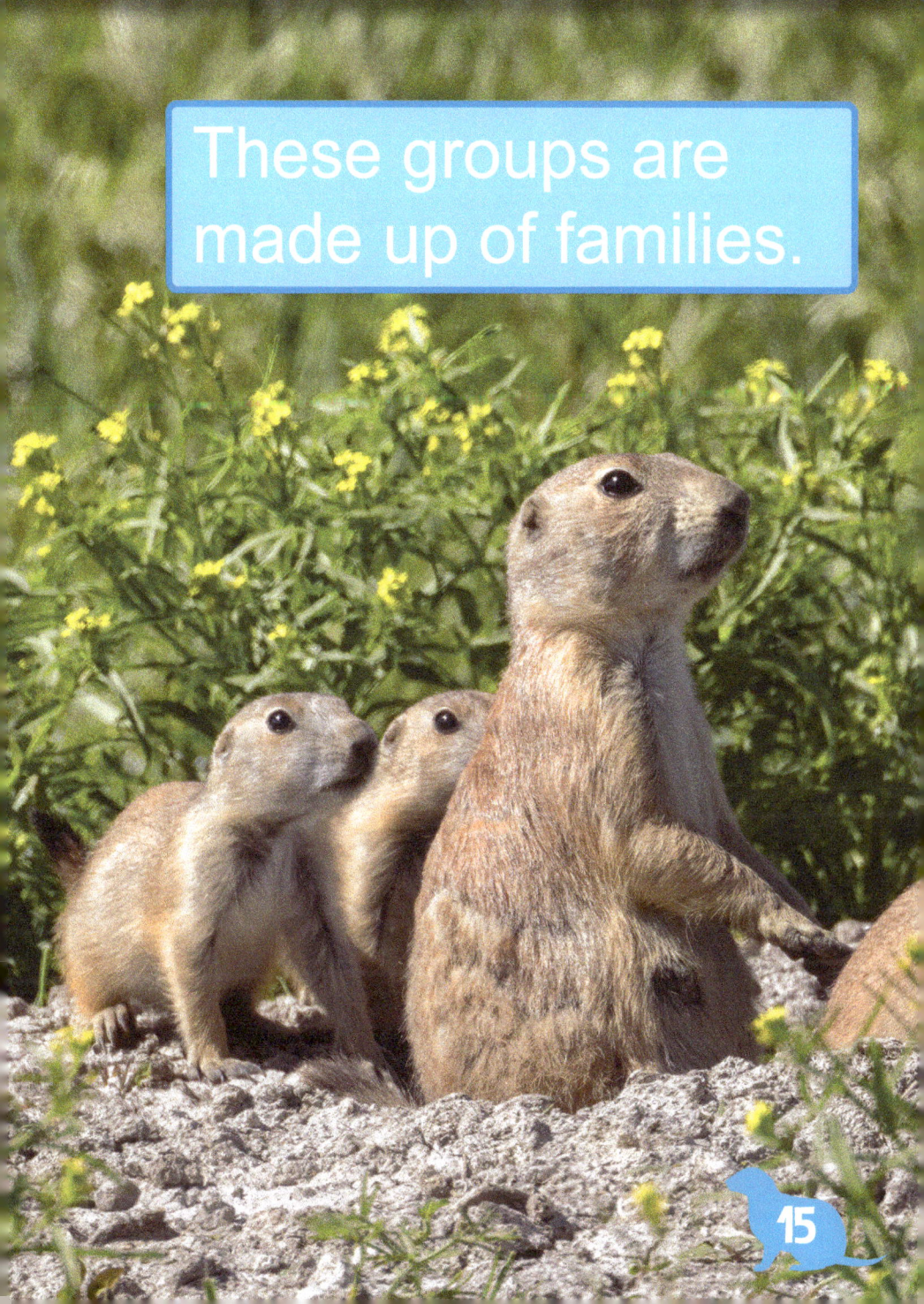

Prairie dog groups dig tunnels underground.

Each family has their own space.

Prairie dogs guard their tunnels.

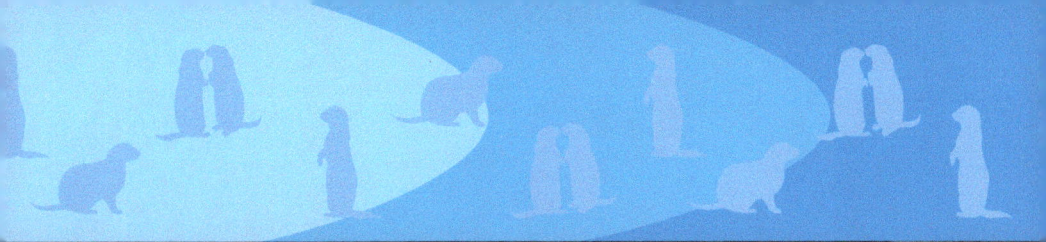

They stand on their back feet by the opening.

Prairie dogs will bark
if danger gets close.

This tells other prairie
dogs to hide.

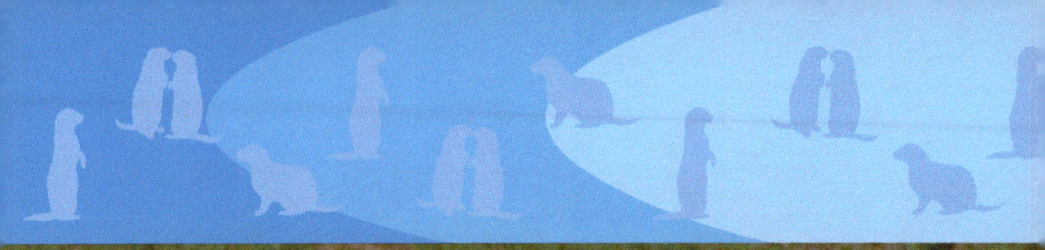

Digging tunnels helps make soil healthy.

This helps plants grow.

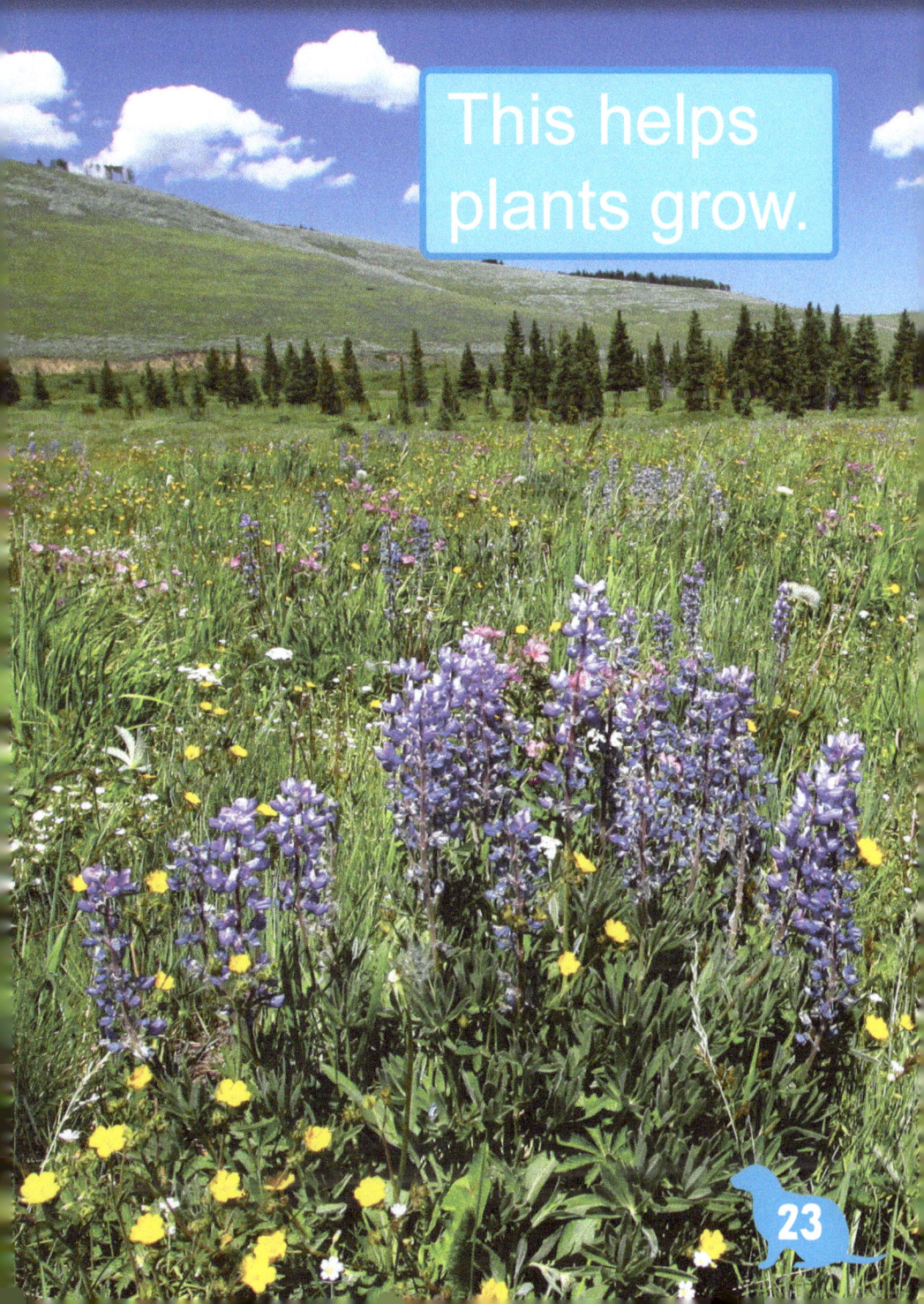

23

Prairie dog tunnels help other animals too.

Other animals
sometimes
live in them.

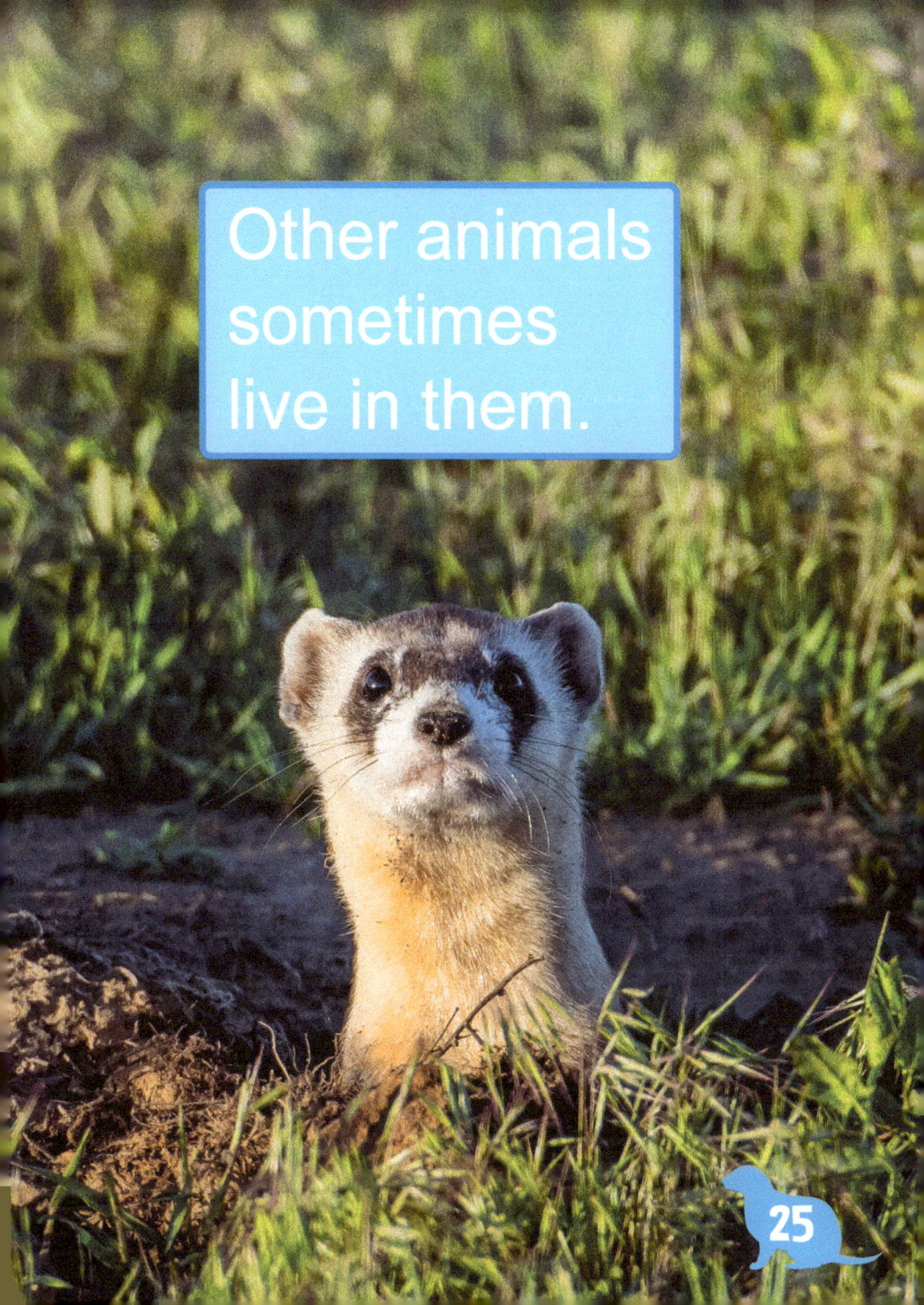

25

Prairie dog babies are called pups.

They are born
without fur.

Pups leave home after about a year.

They live for three
to five years.

# Quiz

Test your knowledge of prairie dogs by answering the following questions. The questions are based on what you have read in this book. The answers are listed on the bottom of the next page.

**1** Do prairie dogs climb trees like other squirrels?

**2** Do prairie dogs eat grass?

**3** Do prairie dogs live in large groups?

**4** Do prairie dogs dig tunnels?

**5** Does digging tunnels help make soil healthy?

**6** Are prairie dogs born with fur?

# Explore other books in the
# *Animals That Make a Difference* series

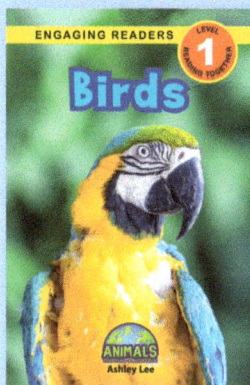

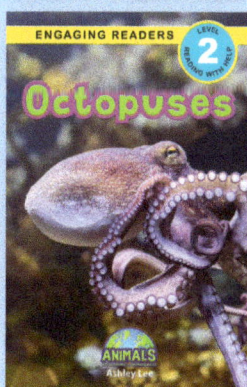

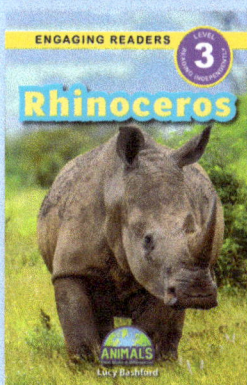

Visit www.engagebooks.com to explore more Engaging Readers.

www.ingramcontent.com/pod-product-compliance
Lightning Source LLC
Chambersburg PA
CBHW052036030426
42337CB00027B/5029

* 9 7 8 1 7 7 8 7 8 7 0 1 0 *